NATURAL WORLD WONDERS

Ann Evans

Badger Publishing Limited
Oldmedow Road,
Hardwick Industrial Estate,
King's Lynn PE30 4JJ
Telephone: 01553 816083

www.badgerlearning.co.uk

2 4 6 8 10 9 7 5 3 1

Natural World Wonders ISBN: 978-1-78837-569-6

Text © Ann Evans

Complete work © Badger Publishing Limited 2022

All rights reserved. No part of this publication may be reproduced, stored in any form or by any means mechanical, electronic, recording or otherwise without the prior permission of the publisher.

The right of Ann Evans to be identified as author of this work has been asserted by them in accordance with the Copyright, Designs and Patents Act 1988.

Commissioning Editor: Sarah Rudd
Copyeditor: Carrie Lewis
Designer: Adam Wilmott

Cover Shutterstock/Anders Riishede
Page 4: Shutterstock/eskystudio
Page 5: Alamy/Science History Images
Page 6: National Science Foundation/Peter Rejcek via Wikimedia Commons
Page 7: Shutterstock/alejojimenezyt
Page 8: Shutterstock/2630ben
Page 9: Shutterstock/Olga Kot Photo
Page 10: Shutterstock/evenfh
Page 11: Shutterstock/rjmiguel, Nobu Tamura via Wikimedia Commons
Page 12: Shutterstock/HannaTor
Page 13: Shutterstock/Milton Rodriguez
Page 14: Shutterstock/Daniel Prudek
Page 15: Alamy/Keystone Press
Page 16: Shutterstock/D Currin
Page 17: Shuttestock/Zhukova Valentyna
Page 18: Shutterstock/Lane V. Erickson
Page 19: Shutterstock/Mark A Lee
Page 20: Shutterstock/Pelikh Alexey and Shutterstock/Krumpelman Photography
Page 21: Shutterstock/Guitar photographer
Page 22: Shutterstock/Kurit afshen, Juliet Breese
Page 23: Shutterstock/Nynke van Holten, Shutterstock/Adalbert Dragon
Page 24: Shutterstock/Max_Lockwood
Page 25: Shutterstock/Maciej Bledowski
Page 26: Shutterstock/ProDesign studio
Page 27: Shutterstock/Dmitry Leonov
Page 28: Shutterstock/4kclips
Page 29: Shutterstock/JamiesOnAMission

Every effort has been made to contact copyright holders of material reproduced in this book. Any omissions will be rectified in subsequent printings if notice is given to the publisher.

NATURAL WORLD WONDERS

Contents

1. Wonderful Waterfalls	4
2. Fantastic Flatlands	9
3. Magnificent Mountains	13
4. Vast Valleys and Hills	17
5. Fabulous Forests	21
6. Lagoons, Lakes and Coral Reefs	26
Glossary	30
Questions	31
Index	32

Badger
LEARNING

1. Wonderful Waterfalls

Waterfalls are one of the most beautiful natural wonders in the world. They were once worshipped as magical places and people are still drawn to these amazing marvels today.

Words highlighted in this colour are in the glossary on page 30

Niagara Falls

Niagara Falls is actually made of three separate waterfalls: American Falls, Bridal Veil Falls and Horseshoe Falls.

One side of Niagara Falls is in Canada, the other side is in the state of New York, USA. The height ranges between 51 and 53.6 metres.

Around 12 million tourists visit Niagara every year.

The Great Blondin crossing the Niagara Falls on a tightrope, carrying his manage on his shoulders.

In 1859, a French acrobat called Charles Blondin crossed Niagara on a tightrope. His stunts got more daring – tightrope walking while blindfolded, while pushing a wheelbarrow, stopping for a glass of wine and even cooking an omelette. These days such stunts are banned.

Blood Falls

Blood Falls is a waterfall in Antarctica. Although it looks gruesome, it is not actual blood!

It is very salty water, containing iron, which bubbles up from underground water sources. When the water mixes with the oxygen in the air it **oxidises**, turning the iron rusty-red colour.

The water has been hidden beneath the glacier for five million years. Scientists study this area and the unusual conditions. Their research may even help us understand about possible life on other planets.

Angel Falls

Angel Falls in Venezuela is the tallest waterfall in the world. It is 979 metres high – this is equal to three Eiffel Towers!

The waterfall and mountains are millions of years old. Local Pemón Indians call the Angel Falls *Kerepakupai Merú*, which means 'leap from the deepest place'.

In 1935, American pilot James Crawford Angel discovered the waterfall whilst flying and searching for gold. In 1937, he crash-landed his plane on the marshy mountain top. James, his wife and two others descended the mountain on foot and it took 11 days for them to reach civilisation. The waterfall is named after him.

WOW! facts

James Angel's monoplane remained on the mountain top for 33 years before being air-lifted to a museum by helicopter. James Angel died in 1960 and his ashes were scattered over the falls.

Victoria Falls

Victoria Falls is a waterfall on the Zambezi River in southern Africa. It is the largest sheet of falling water in the world and one of the World's Seven Natural Wonders.

At low water times you can swim to the edge of the Falls at Devil's Pool. It is quite safe, but watch out for the hippos and crocodiles!

WOW! facts

Every minute, 500 million litres of water cascade over the edge of Victoria Falls. That's the same as 200 olympic-sized swimming pools emptying every 60 seconds.

2. Fantastic Flatlands

There are magnificent flatlands to be found all over the Earth. Some of these landscapes are so strange they look as if they could be on another planet.

Salar de Uyuni

In the wet season, the whole 10,000 square kilometres of Salar de Uyuni, Bolivia, turns into the world's largest mirror.

WOW! facts
This strange landscape was the location for planet Crait in the movie *Star Wars: The Last Jedi*.

The Namib Desert

At 55 million years old, the Namib Desert in Namibia is one of the world's oldest deserts. Its sand dunes are the tallest on the planet.

Temperatures can reach 60 degrees Celsius in the daytime and fall to zero at night. Around 3500 species of plants and many large animals live in these **arid** conditions – even elephants.

The Sahara Desert

The Sahara Desert is the largest hot desert in the world. It is located in North Africa and spans across 11 different countries. The Sahara covers 3.6 million square miles – that is just a little smaller than all of the USA!

The only people living in the Sahara Desert are Bedouin **nomads** who move around on camels. Finding water is difficult. There are 20 lakes in the Sahara Desert and all contain saltwater except one.

WOW! facts

The Sahara hasn't always been a desert. Lots of dinosaur fossils have been found here, including an 80-million-year-old Mansourasaurus. It's thought to have been ten metres long and weigh 5000 kilograms.

Badwater Basin

Badwater Basin is in Death Valley National Park, USA. These salt flats are the lowest point in the USA at 85.5 metres below sea level.

You need to walk a mile across the salt crystals before coming to the strange hexagonal patterns formed by the salt. These patterns are constantly shifting and changing.

WOW! facts

An early **surveyor** came through the salt flats on his mule looking for water. When he finally came across some, his mule refused to drink it. This is how the area became known as 'Badwater Basin'.

3. Magnificent Mountains

Although some people want to climb a mountain, others are happy to just look and admire these natural wonders.

Rainbow Mountains

The Rainbow Mountains in northwest China are 200 square miles of vivid rainbow colours. They are one of the most beautiful landforms in China.

WOW! facts

There are more rainbow mountains in Peru which were only discovered when the snow that was covering them melted due to climate change.

The Rainbow Mountains in China.

Mount Everest

Mount Everest, located between Nepal and Tibet, is the world's highest mountain above sea level at 8849 metres. Temperatures can drop as low as -42 degrees Celsius and winds of more than 100 miles per hour can hit the mountain.

WOW! facts

Over 300 people have died trying to reach Mount Everest's peak. Many bodies still lie frozen in the ice as it is too dangerous to retrieve them.

The first known people to have **conquered** Everest were Edmund Hillary, a New Zealand mountaineer, and Tenzing Norgay, a Sherpa from Nepal. In 1953, they began to climb the mountain and after seven weeks they finally reached the summit.

Annapurna

Annapurna in Nepal is the deadliest mountain in the world with a 29 per cent mortality rate. This means that for nearly every three people that go up the mountain, one of them will die.

Mount Kilimanjaro

Mount Kilimanjaro in Tanzania is often called 'The Roof of Africa' as it towers over the African continent. It contains a **dormant** volcano which may erupt again one day, even though it has not erupted for 200,000 years.

There are eight trails up Kilimanjaro, which can all be hiked without special climbing gear. About 110,000 climbers attempt to reach the summit each year but only half of these succeed.

WOW! facts

The oldest person to successfully climb Kilimanjaro was Anne Lorimor at age 89. The youngest person was only six years old.

4. Vast Valleys and Hills

Earth's **geology** has left a lasting mark on the landscapes we see. The paths made by moving water and ice have made many unique shapes in the landscape, whilst volcanoes and earthquakes have left us with peaks and jagged rocks.

Grand Canyon

The Grand Canyon was formed around six million years ago and is made up of enormous red rocks, deep valleys, dense forests, raging rivers and wild rapids. It is located in Arizona, USA and is 277 miles long – that's about the length of 4500 football pitches!

WOW! facts

Since the mid-1800s there have been more than 770 deaths in the Grand Canyon, including being struck by lightning to murders.

Yellowstone National Park

Yellowstone, USA, was the world's first national park. On 1st March 1872, American President U.S. Grant made a new law to protect this one million acre site for future generations to enjoy.

Yellowstone measures 3500 square miles – that's about half the size of Wales. It has canyons, rivers, forests, hot springs, **geysers** and **mud pots**.

One geyser, nicknamed Old Faithful, erupts around 17 times a day. The water can spurt up to 56 metres into the air, which is half as tall as Big Ben!

Yellowstone is home to all kinds of wildlife, from bears and wolves to bison and antelope. Herds of bison have lived here since prehistoric times, and they often bring traffic to a standstill in the park.

WOW! facts

Beneath Yellowstone National Park is a massive super-volcano, possibly the biggest one on Earth. It has been 70,000 years since its last lava flow, but experts believe it will erupt again one day.

Chocolate Hills

Unfortunately, the Chocolate Hills in the Philippines are not made of chocolate. They are 1700 unique formations of grassy hills spread over 50 square kilometres. In the wet season, they are lush and green. In the dry season, this fades and the hills turn chocolate-brown.

Giant's Causeway

The Giant's Causeway on the coast of Northern Ireland is made up of 40,000 **basalt** columns – the result of an ancient volcanic eruption.

The tops of the columns form hexagonal stepping-stones. The tallest column is 12 metres high. Some structures have been weathered into strange shapes and given nicknames such as the Giant's Boot, the Camel's Hump and the Chimney Stacks.

5. Fabulous Forests

Full of life and mystery, forests have been around for hundreds of millions of years. They provide a rich environment for both animals and humans to live.

Bamboo forests

Forests of bamboo cover huge areas in Asia, Africa, Central America and South America. There are around 1400 different species of bamboo and it is the fastest growing plant in the world. Some species can grow up to 91 centimetres per day.

The Sagano Bamboo Forest, Japan, is the country's most famous and beautiful bamboo forest. It covers 16 kilometres and contains a giant type of bamboo that can reach up to 28 metres high.

Amazon rainforest

The Amazon is the world's largest rainforest with over half of it growing in Brazil, but it stretches across nine different countries. It covers 2.1 million square miles – this is twice the size of India. It's hot and humid and rains most days.

A third of the world's flowering plants live in the Amazon, which is around 80,000 different species, as well as 16,000 species of tree and 2.5 million species of insects!

The Amazon can be a dangerous place! Jaguars, pumas, South American rattlesnakes, boa constrictors, the green anaconda and piranhas all live in the dense undergrowth and rivers.

WOW! facts

Around 400 tribes of **indigenous** people live in the Amazon rainforest, which is over one million people. Some have had little contact with the world outside.

Redwood National Park

The Redwood National Park on the coast of California, USA, covers 562 square kilometres. Before 1850 there were more than 8000 square kilometres of redwood forest but during the gold rush about 90 per cent were cut down for wood.

Fortunately, in 1968, a law to protect the Redwood National Park was brought in.

WOW! facts

Redwood trees can grow to over 90 metres and live for hundreds of years. The current tallest tree reaches almost 116 metres. The oldest tree is 3200 years old. Its location is a secret.

Crooked Forest

The Crooked Forest in Poland is a strange **grove** of weirdly shaped pine trees.

The 400 trees were planted around 1930 in 22 lines. They were between seven and ten years old when something happened to make them bend in an odd way.

Some people say heavy snow fall affected the trees when they were saplings. Others say locals tried to shape them for furniture or ship building. Maybe tanks drove through the forest during World War Two and crushed the young trees. Really, no one knows and the Crooked Forest remains a mystery.

6. Lagoons, Lakes and Coral Reefs

The most unexplored landscapes on Earth are those that are underwater but here are some of the wonders discovered so far.

The Great Barrier Reef

The Great Barrier Reef is located off the coast of Australia and is one of World's Seven Natural Wonders.

It is the world's largest coral reef, stretching for over 2300 kilometres, which is over twice the length of the United Kingdom! It is home to thousands of plants, marine life and bird species, many of them endangered.

Lake Retba

Lake Retba, in northwest Africa, is separated from the Atlantic Ocean by a narrow strip of sand dunes but because it is so close to the ocean, it has a very high salt content. This attracts a bacteria which gives the lake its unique pink colour. Sometimes when salt levels rise to 40 per cent the lake looks blood red!

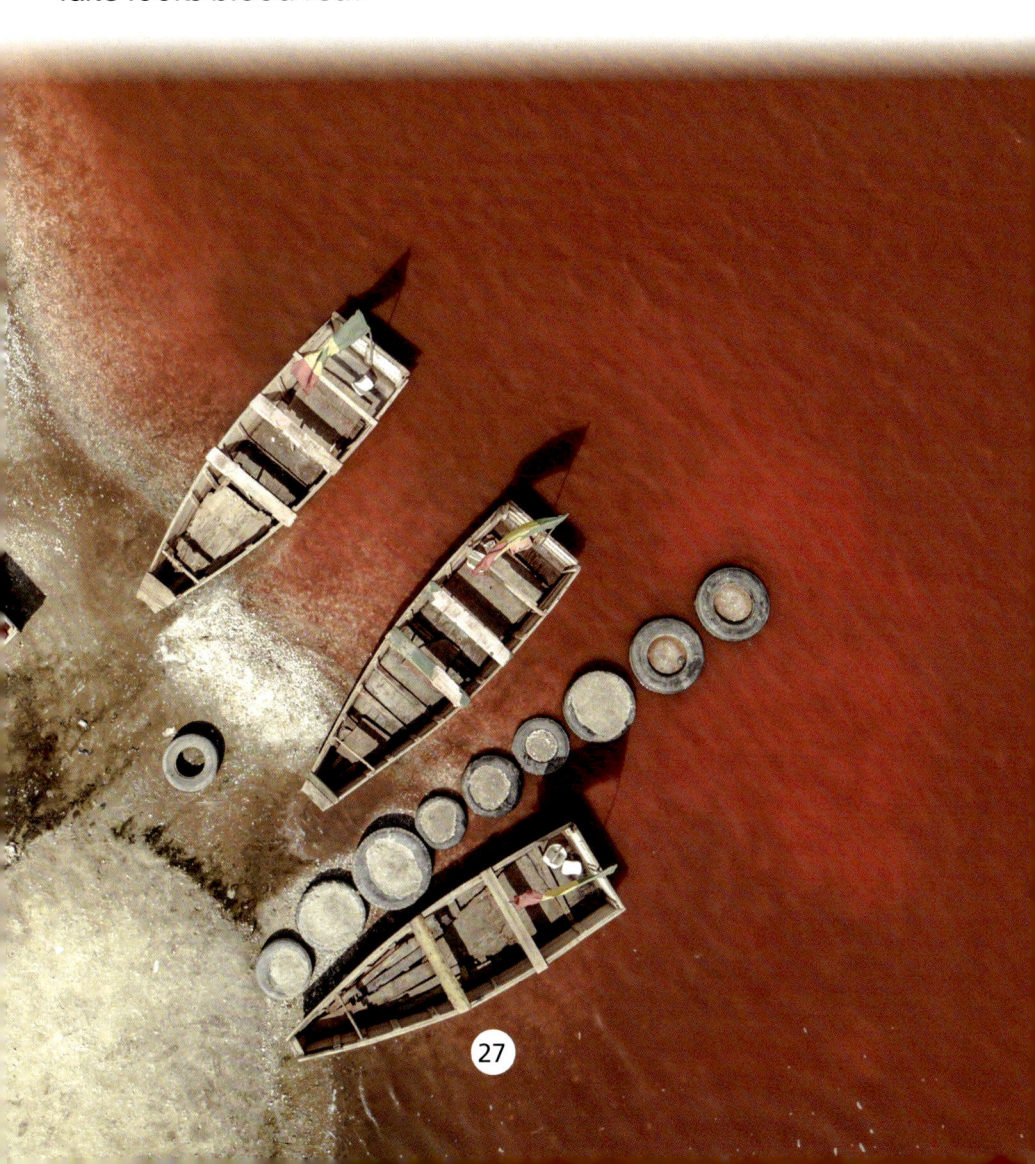

Loch Ness

Loch Ness in the Scottish Highlands is famous for its sightings of the Loch Ness Monster – *Nessie*. There have been over 1000 eye-witness accounts of Nessie since a photo was shown to the world in 1933, but no one has ever proven the monster exists.

Loch Ness is 37 kilometres in length, but in places it is 243 metres deep. The volume of water in Loch Ness is a staggering 7.4 billion cubic metres. This is enough space for every single person on earth to fit inside ten times over!

The Great Blue Hole

Blue holes can be found in oceans all around the world. They are large sinkholes, caused by the collapse of underwater caves.

They are called blue holes because of the distinct contrast of the dark blue in the deep-water area, compared to the lighter blue of the shallow water.

The Great Blue Hole near Belize is 124 metres deep and 318 metres across. It was caused by an underwater cave collapsing 15,000 years ago.

WOW! facts

The Great Blue Hole is popular with divers – and with sharks! The Caribbean reef shark, nurse shark, hammerhead shark, bull shark and black tip shark are all found here.

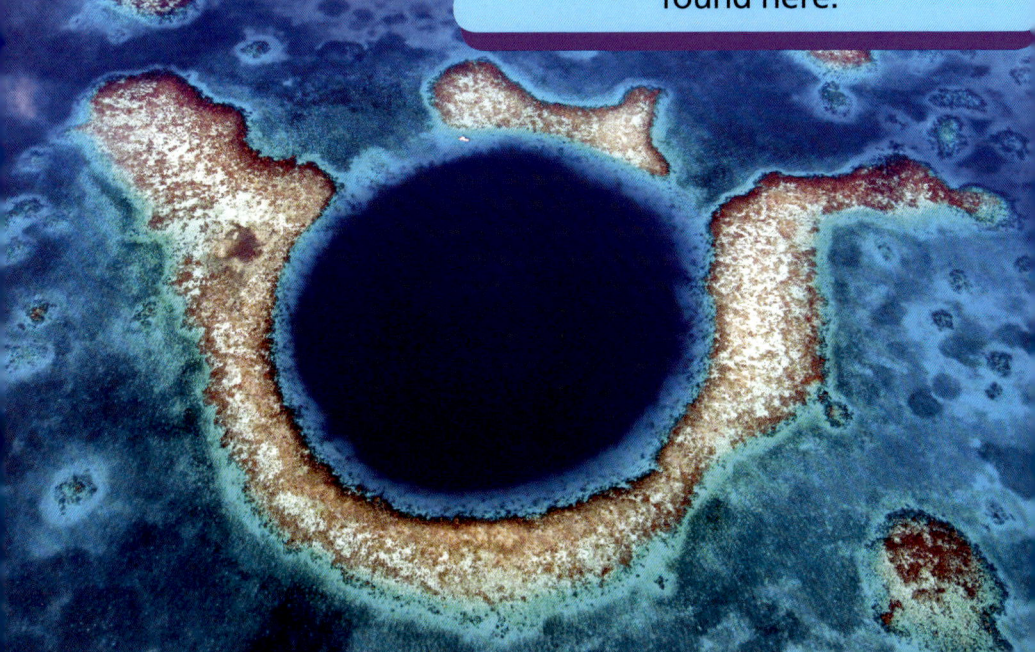

GLOSSARY

arid — having little to no rain

basalt — a type of dark rock that is formed by the cooling of lava

dormant — a type of volcano that has not erupted in the last 10,000 years

geology — study of the rocks and physical processes of earth to understand its origin and history

geysers — a natural pool of hot water that erupts

glacier — a thick mass of ice that covers a large area

grove — a small group of trees

mud pots — a hot spring filled with boiling mud

nomads — a person who moves from place to place with no permanent home

oxidises — to combine with oxygen

reservoirs — a man-made lake used to store water, usually for drinking

surveyor — someone who maps a piece of land

Questions

Who walked over Niagara Falls on a tightrope? *(page 5)*

Where would you find the world's largest natural mirror? *(page 9)*

Which is the world's highest mountain? *(page 14)*

What is Old Faithful? *(page 18)*

In which country is the Crooked Forest? *(page 25)*

How many species of fish can be found in the Great Barrier Reef? *(page 27)*

INDEX

Africa 8, 11, 16, 21, 27
Amazon rainforest 22, 23
Angel Falls 7
Annapurna 15
Antarctica 6
Asia 21
Australia 26
Badwater Basin 12
Belize 29
Blood Falls 6
Bolivia 9
Brazil 22
Canada 4
Charles Blondin 5
China 13
Chocolate Hills 20
Crooked Forest 25
Edmund Hillary 11
Giant's Causeway 20
Grand Canyon 17
Great Barrier Reef 26
Great Blue Hole 29
Japan 21
James Angel 7
Lake Retba 27

Loch Ness 28
Mount Everest 14
Mount Kilimanjaro 16
Namib Desert 10
Namibia 10
Nepal 15
Niagara 4, 5
Northern Ireland 20
Old Faithful 18
Peru 13
Philippines 20
Poland 25
Rainbow Mountains 13
Redwood National Park 24
Sagano Bamboo Forest 21
Sahara Desert 11
Salar de Uyuni 9
South America 21, 23
Tanzania 16
Tenzing Norgay 15
USA 4, 11, 12, 17, 18, 24
Venezuela 7
Victoria Falls 8
Yellowstone 18, 19
Zambezi River 8